MICHELANGELO
AND THE RENAISSANCE

BY

DAVID SPENCE

THE WORLD IN THE 1500S

*A*lthough the year 1500 seems today to be a very long time ago, historians use this date to mark the beginning of what is referred to as modern history. It is an arbitrary date but it does mark the change between the medieval world and the modern world whose values continue today. The High Renaissance, to which Michelangelo belonged, dates from about the year 1500 and was the high point of a change in European history that started about one hundred years earlier in Italy. *Renaissance* means rebirth, and refers to a return to the classical ideals of the ancient Greeks and Romans. The Renaissance was characterized by an increasing independence of thought, which led to the shattering of traditional Christian unity as well as a new curiosity about the world in which people found themselves. The voyages of Columbus opened up the New World of Central and South America to ruthless exploitation by the Spanish and Portuguese who were to follow. Islam spread rapidly through the kingdoms of North Africa. Africa was shrouded in mystery to the Europeans who had begun to establish trading stations on its west coast. Trade routes were becoming established throughout the world, linking the Americas, Europe, India, Asia, and Africa, bringing wealth to new dynasties and changing the lives of millions of people.

THE GREAT AND HIDDEN CONTINENT

Africa was cut off from European explorers by the Sahara Desert until the maritime nations, such as Portugal, started trading with West African kingdoms like Benin. It was from this time that the slave trade began to grow.

RELIGIOUS REVOLUTION

Martin Luther was a German monk who demanded the reform of the Catholic Church, which he saw as corrupt. His followers, the reformers, started a movement that became known as the Reformation. In 1521 Luther was expelled from the Church because of his protests. He set up his own Church, which became known as the Lutheran, one of the Protestant Churches.

THE POWER OF THE CROWN

Nowhere was the growing power of the monarchy more clearly felt than in England. European countries developed nation states ruled by kings who had absolute power over their people. The French kings were portrayed as Roman emperors, "Kings by the grace of God, not by election or force." The maritime empires of Spain and Portugal were becoming established and were to dominate world trade during the course of the sixteenth century. Henry VIII, king of England from 1509 to 1547, challenged the power of the Church of Rome by establishing a new Church in England. In 1533 Henry became Supreme Head of the Church of England.

THE PROGRESS OF SCIENCE

The sciences advanced faster in the sixteenth century than they had at any point in history. The study of natural sciences became systematic and was based on investigation such as Vesalius's first exact descriptions of the human body. Leonardo da Vinci formed theories about the circulation of the blood and made detailed anatomical studies of the human form in a true spirit of inquiry.

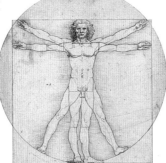

SPREADING THE WORD

The development of the printing press permitted the rapid spread of ideas and had a profound impact on society. Gutenberg's printing process, developed in the fifteenth century, caused a growing revolution as numerous identical copies of words and pictures could be made quickly and cheaply. One example of the impact of printing was that people no longer depended upon one interpretation of the Scriptures, but could study them for themselves.

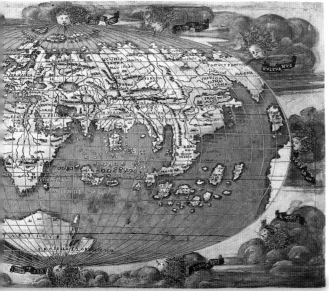

A NEW VIEW OF THE WORLD IN ABOUT 1508

COPERNICUS

The Polish monk Copernicus proved that the earth revolved around the sun rather than the sun around the earth. This discovery was revolutionary at a time when everyone believed that the earth was at the center of the universe. Because of this, Copernicus was terrified of making his discovery known.

THE WORLD OF MICHELANGELO

ichelangelo was born on March 6, 1475 in Caprese, Italy, a small town north of Arezzo, but moved to Florence with his family when barely a month old. It was a time of great change in Italy, which was made up of small states continually struggling for more power and territory. Most of the inhabitants depended on the land for their livelihood. The one means of fast progression was through the all-powerful Church of Rome, which offered a means of escape from the drudgery of peasant life. Michelangelo benefited greatly from the patronage of the Church and received all of his greatest commissions from Church sources. However, the great changes in the Church during Michelangelo's lifetime were a result of the deep corruption that had grown unchecked over many years. Italy suffered devastation at the hands of invading armies at the turn of the century. The French invaded in 1494, when Michelangelo was nineteen years old, and the Spanish took Rome in 1527. These great upheavals must have affected Michelangelo as they did so many of his fellow countrymen and women.

LORENZO THE MAGNIFICENT

The Medici family was enormously powerful and rich, making their money in banking and exerting their power by ruling Florence for over 300 years. Lorenzo de'Medici, who was in power at the time Michelangelo was growing up in Florence, owned a collection of broken antique pillars and stone figures, which were kept in the garden of San Marco. Lorenzo de'Medici allowed artists to study the antique sculptures. The young Michelangelo was allowed to work there while staying in the Medici household. Lorenzo de'Medici undoubtedly saw great talent in Michelangelo and helped his career as an artist. Lorenzo died in 1492 and was succeeded by his son Pier de'Medici, continuing the family line.

THE LEARNED ARCHITECT

The buildings of Donato Bramante displayed great learning and knowledge of the classical builders of antiquity. His buildings, such as the famous church of St. Peter's in Rome, were originally designed to compete with famous ancient ruins such as the Pantheon, but Bramante's designs were too extravagant for the Church's purse. Nevertheless, the harmonious classical forms of his buildings, such as the Tempietto in Rome, embody the Renaissance ideals of order and symmetry. Michelangelo praised Bramante, saying he was "... as worthy an architect as any since ancient times."

ISABELLA D'ESTE

Isabella d'Este was a woman of great learning who became a patron of the Renaissance arts, employing people such as the artist Correggio and the writer Castiglione, whose books popularized humanist philosophy. Humanism, led by the Dutch philosopher Erasmus, was an important movement of the Renaissance. Its central belief was that human reason was more important than religious doctrine and, like other Renaissance movements, referred to classical studies. Isabella d'Este's fame in Italy is evident by the number of portraits that exist by artists such as Leonardo da Vinci and this one by Titian.

SNOWMAN

It is said that Lorenzo the Magnificent's son, Pier de'Medici, did not recognize the value of the creative genius of Michelangelo as his father had. The story goes that in a frivolous mood, Pier ordered Michelangelo to make a snowman in the courtyard of the Medici palace. From this moment, Michelangelo realized his future might be better—and safer— elsewhere, and moved from Florence to Bologna. This move was wise for a reason Michelangelo could not have known: in 1494 Charles VIII of France, with a sizable army, invaded Italy and took the city of Florence.

NICCOLÒ MACHIAVELLI

The Florentine statesman and political philosopher is remembered chiefly for his book written in 1532 entitled *Il Principe* (The Prince). This study of political power concluded that those in power must be prepared to use any means necessary to achieve their goals. Machiavelli's name has become associated with political deviousness, but that is largely the result of subsequent criticism by the Church.

THE ART OF HIS DAY

T he Renaissance was a rebirth that led to new ways of thinking in the sciences, philosophy, and architecture, as well as in painting and sculpture. It rejected the recent medieval past with its Gothic art and architecture and returned to the golden ages of the great Greek and Roman civilizations. The Renaissance movement in art spanned several centuries but was at its greatest during the time of Michelangelo. The artist Giotto, who lived and worked in Florence between 1267 and 1337, is today known as the father of Western painting because of his method of representing figures and landscapes with great realism and in a naturalistic style. Giotto's influence on later painters, particularly Masaccio, carried forward the sculptural realism and solidity of form that exemplified Renaissance painting and which culminated in the monumental figures of Michelangelo.

BRONZE PUTTO

Verrocchio

Renaissance art often included naked children with wings depicting cupids and angels. This was a fashion borrowed from the ancient Greeks and Romans. *Putto* is Italian for little boy. The plural is *putti*.

CRUCIFIXION

Grünewald

Although painted at the same time as Raphael's *School of Athens,* the difference in artistic approach to the paintings could not have been greater. Matthias Grünewald was a German contemporary of Raphael who ignored the influence of the Renaissance, choosing a deeply religious theme and working in a way that bears a greater resemblance to the medieval Gothic style filled with darkness and suffering. The painting was commissioned by the Antonite Monastery Hospital at Isenheim near Strasbourg, which cared for plague victims. The intention of the painting was to give comfort to the dying by reinforcing their religious faith. Grünewald portrays Christ's body covered by sores because he felt this would help the plague victims to relate Christ's situation to their own.

THE SCHOOL OF ATHENS

Raphael

Raphael was working in Florence at the same time as Michelangelo and Leonardo, but his career was cut short by his death in 1520 when he was thirty-seven years old. In his lifetime Raphael was considered to be an artist of equal stature to both Michelangelo and Leonardo, despite being thirty-one years younger than Leonardo. Raphael's great achievement was to create harmonious compositions including figures that appear to be full of graceful movement. When Raphael was twenty-five years old, he was commissioned by Pope Julius II to decorate the room in the Vatican named the Stanza della Segnatura. In true Renaissance tradition, this fresco is dedicated to the great classical philosophers. At the center of the painting stand Plato and Aristotle. Portrayed around them are Ptolemy, Euclid, Pythagoras, Socrates, and others.

THE VIRGIN OF THE ROCKS

Leonardo da Vinci

One of the most famous names in the history of art, Leonardo da Vinci was a contemporary of Michelangelo. Leonardo's interests spread far beyond painting. His notebooks revealed the extent of his interests, including sketches of mechanical inventions such as tanks and even helicopters. He wrote a treatise on painting that described perspective and how to use an artistic device known as *trompe l'oeil* (pictures that deceive the eye).

DETAIL FROM THE BIRTH OF VENUS *Botticelli*

Painted in Michelangelo's home town of Florence in 1484, Sandro Botticelli's famous painting caused a sensation because it was an important commission that chose to deal with a mythological rather than a religious subject. It dealt with one of the Renaissance's favorite subjects, classical mythology, depicting the birth of the goddess Venus. Botticelli represented Venus as an ideal of classical female beauty. Renaissance artists began to idealize the model. They used an imagined type of model formed from classical statues and improved on nature rather than representing it.

THE FEATURES OF MICHELANGELO

The *Pietà* of 1550, made when Michelangelo was 75 years old, is actually a *deposition,* which refers to the taking down of the dead Christ from the cross. The cowled head of Nicodemus, who is said to have carried Christ's body, is thought to be sculpted on Michelangelo's own features.

FAMILY, FRIENDS, AND OTHERS

Michelangelo was the second of five sons born to Lodovico and Francesca Buonarroti. The 490 surviving letters that Michelangelo wrote over the course of his nearly ninety years to his family, friends, and patrons provide a valuable insight into the life of Michelangelo and of Renaissance Italy. When Michelangelo was in Rome in 1509, he corresponded with his father over money matters—his father had begun to depend upon Michelangelo's income—and his brothers' careers. In June 1509 he wrote: "Dearest father. I realize from your last letter how things are going there and how Giovansimone is behaving... I thought I had arranged matters for them, namely how they might hope to set up a good workshop with my help, as I promised them, and in this hope might apply themselves to becoming proficient and learning their trade, so as to be able to run the shop when the time came." Michelangelo wrote to his wayward brother the same month: "Giovansimone. They say that if you treat a good man kindly you make him even better, and if you treat a wicked man so you make him worse... I am not saying you are wicked, but the way you are carrying on, you never ever please me, or the others. - Let me tell you that you have nothing of your own in this world, and your spending money and your home expenses are what I give you. - If I hear anything more about the way you behave, I'll ride with the post all the way to Florence to show you your mistake..."

FRIEND OR ENEMY?

Raphael of Urbino was a contemporary of Michelangelo who learned a great deal from the master. There was some rivalry between them. Michelangelo is reported to have said that all the misunderstandings he had with Pope Julius II were the result of the envy of Raphael and Bramante. However, Raphael was a great admirer of Michelangelo's art.

TRUE LOVE?

Michelangelo had many close friends but he was never married. Letters and poems written by Michelangelo show that he was very close to Tommaso Cavalieri, who he met in Rome when he was in his fifties and Tommaso in his twenties. Tommaso was known to be an extremely handsome youth and Michelangelo was attracted by his beauty, making many drawings of him. Their friendship lasted until Michelangelo's death. Tommaso inherited many of Michelangelo's drawings, which are now lost. This drawing, entitled *Divine Head,* represents an idealized notion of beauty rather than one drawn from life. It was made when Michelangelo first met Tommaso and may have been based on his friend rather than on his imagination.

FRIENDSHIP

In 1536, while he was working on *The Last Judgment* fresco in the Sistine Chapel, Michelangelo met the Marchioness of Pescara, Vittoria Colonna. Vasari tells that he "greatly loved the Marchioness of Pescara, with whose divine spirits he fell in love." If Tommaso Cavalieri represented physical beauty then Vittoria, widow of the Marquis who died at the battle of Pavia eleven years earlier, represented spiritual beauty; she had devoted herself to religion after her husband's death. It is thought that the woman with the orange veil who is at the feet of Mary in *The Last Judgment* is a portrait of Vittoria. Michelangelo devoted many sonnets to Vittoria. This is an exerpt from "A l'alto tuo lucente diadema":

"My strength is failing me, I spend
my breath half-way - I fall, I stray.
and yet your beauty makes me happy
and nothing else can please my heart
in love with everything sublime
but that, descending here to me
on earth, you are not set apart."

Michelangelo was distraught when she died, forever regretting that when she was dying he did not kiss her brow or face, only her hand.

THE LIFE OF MICHELANGELO

~1475~
Michelangelo di Lodovico di Lionardo di Buonarroto Simoni (Michelangelo) born on March 6 in Caprese, Italy near Arezzo, second of five children.
The family moved to Florence when Michelangelo was a month old.

~1481~
Michelangelo's mother, Francesca, died when he was six years old.

~1488~
Apprenticed to fresco painter Domenico Ghirlandaio in Florence for three years.

~1489–1490~
Studied sculpture in the San Marco garden owned by the Medicis under Bertoldo di Giovanni. Michelangelo impressed and became acquainted with Lorenzo "The Magnificent" de'Medici.

~1492~
Lorenzo de'Medici's death.

~1494~
Moved to Bologna away from Pier de'Medici who had succeeded Lorenzo.

~1496~
Michelangelo moved to Rome and undertook commissions. Sculpted the *Pietà* for Cardinal Lagraulas.

~1501~
Returned to Florence, which was now declared a republic.

~1504~
Carved the statue *David,* which was installed in the main square of Florence.

WHAT DO THE PAINTINGS SAY?

THE SISTINE CHAPEL CEILING

The painting of the ceiling of the Sistine Chapel in Rome is without doubt one of the greatest feats ever accomplished and this work alone is enough to have carried Michelangelo's name across the centuries as a giant among artists. The scale is breathtaking; the impact overwhelming; yet this work was accomplished by Michelangelo virtually single-handedly in about four years, from 1508 to 1512. It is no wonder that Michelangelo's contemporaries called him the divine Michelangelo. The frescoes cover approximately 5,800 square feet across the barrel-vaulted ceiling of the barn-like building of the chapel, which stands next to the Vatican. Michelangelo was commissioned by Pope Julius II in 1505 and was given, according to the artist, a free hand to design whatever he wanted.

The central area of the ceiling is made up of nine panels showing scenes from the Old Testament of the Bible, beginning with three about the Creation, three on Adam and Eve, and three on the story of Noah. They are surrounded by figures of *sibyls* (prophetesses

THE DRUNKENNESS OF NOAH

The Old Testament tells how Noah, who owned vineyards, became drunk and lay naked. His son Ham covers his father while his brothers Japheth and Shem look away.

THE FLOOD

This panel tells the well-known story of the Flood that will drown all the people, while Noah and his family climb aboard the Ark.

THE SACRIFICE

Noah builds an altar in thanksgiving for being saved, and makes an offering to God. God blesses Noah and his family.

in Greek mythology) and Hebrew prophets. The design is linked by athletic male figures (*ignudi*) who hold bronze medallions and also serve to link the Christian stories with classical antiquity.

The first three panels created by Michelangelo deal with the story of Noah and were painted in the order shown here, although they are of course intended to be viewed in reverse starting with the Creation at the altar end of the chapel.

The middle three panels show the Fall, Adam and Eve:

THE FALL

Eve takes the apple from the serpent and Adam and Eve are expelled from the Garden of Eden.

THE CREATION OF EVE

God bids the figure of Eve arise from beside the slumbering Adam.

THE CREATION OF ADAM

This panel shows Adam just as he is about to receive the charge of life from God.

The final three panels deal with the Creation:

GOD SEPARATING EARTH FROM WATER

The swirling, powerful figure of God creates the firmament.

THE CREATION OF THE SUN, MOON AND STARS

An awesome, bearded God is shown in the act of creation, throwing the Sun and Moon into their positions in the universe.

GOD SEPARATING LIGHT FROM DARKNESS

God cleaves the clouds of darkness, bringing forth light.

THE CREATION OF ADAM

This image is one of the greatest icons of Western art. Michelangelo has depicted Adam as if just awakened and about to be charged with the energy of life through the outstretched arm of God, who is borne aloft by a cloud of angels. The beginning of human history starts with this moment, captured brilliantly by Michelangelo. It is the anticipation of the moment that gives the painting its tension and vitality; Michelangelo is revealing the story to us even before it begins.

LIFE-GIVING ENERGY

The eyes of Adam, God, and the angels all focus intently on the outstretched hand of God and the hand of Adam. The viewer can tell that the moment is about to happen because of the smallest of gaps that remains between the two fingers, and from the fact that Adam's hand is supine; the life-giving energy has not yet passed from one to the other.

THE BURDEN OF MORTALITY

By comparing the face of Eve before and after eating the fruit, it is possible to see the consequences of her action. Her face is young and beautiful beforehand, but is creased and lined with the burden of mortality as she walks away from the Garden.

THE FALL

This picture is divided into two separate scenes. The left-hand scene shows Adam and Eve in the Garden of Eden. Eve reaches out behind her to take the forbidden fruit, which is offered to her by the serpent from the Tree of Knowledge. The serpent is depicted as half woman, half snake, and reflects the male-dominated interpretation of the story by casting the woman in the role of temptress. The Tree of Knowledge around which the serpent is wound acts as a divider between the left-hand scene and the right, which shows the expulsion of Adam and Eve from the Garden of Eden. God banishes them because, having eaten of the Tree of Knowledge, they know Good and Evil, and if they stay and eat of the Tree of Life they will live forever. The angel with the sword refers to the "flaming sword" that God placed east of Eden to guard the entrance to the Garden.

STORIES FROM THE SISTINE CHAPEL

*I*nterpretations of the ceiling frescoes differ, but the subject matter may have been partly based on the decorations that were already in place when Michelangelo started his work. Michelangelo signed his contract on May 10, 1508 and was to be paid 3,000 ducats, which was quickly doubled to 6,000 ducats. Work started in July 1508 and continued until 1510, when Michelangelo traveled to Bologna, apparently to persuade the Pope to provide more money.

Giorgio Vasari's *Life of Michelangelo* tells that one day the impatient Pope asked when he would finish, to which Michelangelo replied "When I'm able to." The Pope, infuriated, continued: "You want me to have you thrown off that scaffolding now, don't you?" The ceiling was finally completed in 1512 and unveiled on All Saints' Day. Michelangelo's letter at the time records: "I have finished the chapel which I was painting; the Pope is very satisfied; and the other matters are not turning out as I wished but these times are very unfavorable to our art."

THE LIBYAN SIBYL

Sibyl is the Hellenistic Greek name given to a prophetess, but also became linked with Old Testament prophets in Christian literature. The most famous sibyl was Cumae (also portrayed on the Sistine Chapel ceiling) who told Aeneas in the *Aeneid* how to enter the underworld. They are supposed to have kept in their possession books of prophecy that could be referred to in times of need. This may explain why Michelangelo depicted the Libyan Sibyl holding open a book. What the viewer sees, however, is a figure who twists to hold open the pages as she balances on tiptoe in her niche in the ceiling. Michelangelo paints the pose with breathtaking confidence and even humor; Sibyl's dress is caught under the block of stone on which she balances.

DAWN AND DUSK AND DAY AND NIGHT

The figures of Lorenzo and Giuliano sit above mythological figures who rest upon the sarcophagi. Beneath the thoughtful Lorenzo lie the female figure of Dawn and male figure of Dusk; beneath the tense Giuliano lie the male figure of Day and female figure of Night. These represent the transient world, whereas the idealized figures of the Medicis show that they have already transcended their material lives and have reached Heaven. This classical pagan symbolism mixes easily with Christian symbolism such as the Madonna and Child to whom the men turn. The female forms are less than convincing when compared to Michelangelo's masterful handling of the male bodies. Nevertheless, the sculptures, with their complex messages about the passing of life and many details that refer to death (rams' skulls, masks, owls, moons, stars, laurels), establish Michelangelo as one of the greatest sculptors ever.

GIULIANO DE'MEDICI

Giuliano, Duke of Nemours, had died in 1516 at the age of thirty-eight. Michelangelo portrays him as alert and ready for action, in military style. He is seated with a baton across his lap, head turned, as if a commander on the point of issuing some instruction to his men.

THE MEDICI CHAPEL

he memoirs of Canon Figiovanni of San Lorenzo, Florence, record that in June 1519 Cardinal Giulio de'Medici said "… we are of a mind to spend about 50,000 ducats on San Lorenzo… which will be called a chapel, where there will be many tombs to bury our dead forefathers: Lorenzo, Giuliano our father, and Giuliano and Lorenzo, brother and nephew." In November 1519 two houses alongside the church of San Lorenzo were demolished to make room for the new chapel, and building commenced on March 1, 1520. The marble from which the tombs were to be carved was ordered from the nearby marble quarry in Carrara. The design for the chapel with its coffered dome reflects the Pantheon, which was a resting place for the famous dead of ancient Rome. Its architecture, however, fuses together the accepted classical style with Michelangelo's own powerful invention, which sometimes contradicts the old rules. Michelangelo completed only two tombs, whose carved figures on two side walls of the chapel look towards a third wall against which stands a sculpture of the Madonna and Child. Opposite the Madonna should have been a third double tomb for Lorenzo the Magnificent and his brother, but work on it was abandoned in 1534 when Michelangelo left Florence for Rome.

LORENZO DE'MEDICI

Lorenzo was only twenty-eight years old when he died in Florence in May 1519, just a few weeks after his wife died in childbirth. Their daughter Catherine survived and eventually became Queen of France. Lorenzo was the last in the direct line of descent from Cosimo de'Medici, and it was his death that prompted the plan to build the chapel. The figure of Lorenzo is depicted with head resting on hand, as if lost in deep thought. Both Lorenzo and Giuliano are portrayed in the classical style of Roman military dress typical of Renaissance art. They are idealized, heroic figures, not true portraits. Michelangelo is reported to have said of the sculptures "In a thousand years' time who will care what they (Lorenzo and Giuliano) really looked like?"

The male figure of Dusk and female figure of Dawn from Lorenzo's tomb.

MICHELANGELO'S PLAN

This sketch with notes in Michelangelo's hand shows the planned double tomb that was to have been for Lorenzo the Magnificent and his brother.

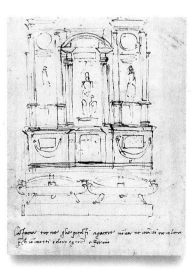

PERSPECTIVE AND PROPORTION

The technical virtuosity of Michelangelo and his fellow artists such as Raphael and Leonardo surpassed anything that had gone before, including the great classical Greek and Roman works that they admired so much. Representation of nature and the human form required methods to make them realistic that we take for granted today. It was not until the 1400s that perspective was truly mastered by artists such as Uccello, creating a sense of depth within the picture. This enabled the artist to create the illusion of three-dimensional objects on a two-dimensional surface such as a flat wall. Michelangelo's twisting human torsos required a complete mastery of foreshortening by which perspective is applied to a single object. An example would be a painted figure whose arm points towards the viewer, showing a great deal of the hand but virtually none of the arm which is behind the hand. (Above) *Painter studying the laws of foreshortening by means of thread and frame.* Woodcut by Durer from the 1525 edition of his book on perspective and proportion.

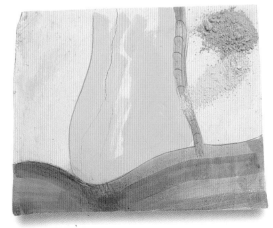

THE PERFECT STONE

The material favored by sculptors in Michelangelo's day was marble. This was the preferred material for carving for thousands of years and remains so today. It is a hard, crystalline rock that is made from limestone and has an extremely fine texture, which permits a highly polished surface. The marble quarries that supplied Michelangelo with his blocks of stone were at Carrara, on the east coast of Italy near Genoa.

A PERMANENT FINISH

The fresco method of painting is absolutely permanent because the pigments mixed with water are absorbed into the still damp surface of the wall. The colors are therefore fixed into the plaster and are less likely to suffer from superficial discoloring or damage.

HOW WERE THEY MADE?

*M*ichelangelo's wall paintings employ a method used for hundreds of years called *fresco,* which is the Italian word for fresh. *Buon fresco* or true fresco, which was practiced in Italy at the time of Michelangelo, was the most permanent form of wall decoration. After the wall to be painted was rough plastered, a coat known as the *arriccio* was applied. It was onto this layer that the outline drawing of the final picture (known as the *cartoon*) was traced and so transferred to the wall. An area that could comfortably be covered by the artist in one day was then covered with another coat of plaster (known as the *intonaco*) onto which the cartoon was redrawn. The artist worked on this damp, fresh plaster by mixing pigments with water that sometimes contained lime. At this stage, the color integrated permanently with the plaster wall. This method required confidence and sureness of touch because once the color was absorbed into the plaster, it was not possible to retouch.

SIMPLE TOOLS

The hammer and chisel were the means by which Michelangelo created his breathtaking sculptures. The claw chisel (top) dug into the stone, producing a grooved surface as if it had been combed. This type of chiseling action gave the artist greater control and prevented the chisel from inadvertently chipping the stone.

ATLAS

This extraordinary figure of Atlas, carved by Michelangelo in about 1520, demonstrates both the power and technique of his art. Atlas appears to be struggling to free his head from a huge block of stone, and is condemned to do so for all eternity. The figure shows how the artist gradually frees the figure by carving into the block.

Modeling

The two main types of sculpture are modeling and carving. Modeling involves building up a shape from soft material such as clay. With modeling, it is possible to change the shape of the object at any time by adding or taking away the material, and the surface and texture can be changed according to the way the soft material is manipulated. After the object is satisfactorily shaped, it is common practice to turn the soft material into a hard one. Clay can be baked in the same way as pottery, and plaster casts can be made, enabling the object to be cast in a permanent material. A process known as lost wax, which has been practiced for thousands of years, uses molten bronze to replace the wax shape and so produce a permanent metal sculpture.

Carving

Carving, Michelangelo's preferred method, involves taking away material from a solid block to reveal a shape in the round. The artist must already have a vision of the shape within the block and carves the block away to reveal the shape. Artists might use different types of stone or wood but marble is often used because of its fine texture, which prevents it from flaking and permits smooth surfaces. Marble is said to have a soft buttery consistency once the external surface has been pierced. Pumice stone (shown here) can be used to rub the surface of the carved marble into a highly polished finish.

In the Round

The most important difference between modeling and carving is that once material is taken away from a block it cannot be replaced, as is possible with a modeling material such as clay. Artists in Michelangelo's day often made small models known as maquettes to help them see the desired final shape before they started carving the stone. These maquettes, which were usually made of wax, were suspended in a tank half full of water. By turning the maquette from one position to another and observing the waterline around it, the sculptor could better understand how to carve into the block.

THE SCULPTURES

Giorgio Vasari was a Tuscan writer and contemporary of Michelangelo whose book *Lives of the Most Eminent Painters, Sculptors and Architects* was first published in 1550. In his account of the life of Michelangelo, he quotes the artist as saying that it is no wonder that he took so well to the stonemason's chisel, because as a baby, his wet nurse was the daughter of a stonemason and had married another. Michelangelo thought the milk from the breast influenced him when he grew up. There can be no doubt that Michelangelo is one of the greatest, if not the greatest, sculptor in the history of art. It is reported that when at the age of twenty-six, he started work on the almost eighteen foot high block of marble that he was to turn into the figure of *David*, he commenced without even making a clay *maquette* (model) first. Michelangelo built a shed around the block of marble, which had lain in a courtyard near the cathedral for nearly a hundred years, abandoned after previous unsuccessful attempts to carve it into a figure by an earlier generation of artists. He had no assistants, but attacked the marble with furious energy, sometimes working continuously for several days and nights, not leaving the shed but snatching a few hours of sleep on the shed floor.

AWAKENING SLAVE

One of the last pieces worked on by the artist, *The Awakening Slave* shows Michelangelo's interest in contrasting rough-hewn and smoothly polished surfaces.

THE PRIDE OF FLORENCE

Michelangelo had already acquired a reputation as a sculptor by the time he made what is perhaps his best known work, the statue of David, the boy king, with sling resting on his shoulder. The work is a masterpiece of Renaissance art, which demonstrates the idealized human form. The figure stands exactly the height of the original block of marble. The rough surface of the two ends of the block can be seen on the base and crown of David's head.

FAMOUS IMAGES

VIRGIN'S HEAD

Some critics have drawn attention to the fact that the Virgin's face has been sculpted in a way that makes her look far too young to be the Mother of Christ. Michelangelo argued that the Virgin could not age because she was so pure. This sculpture, as with all of Michelangelo's work, embodied the idealized human form in the manner of the High Renaissance.

*R*ecords show that on November 19, 1497 Jean Villiers de Lagraulas, a French Cardinal, arranged for Michelangelo to obtain a block of marble from the quarries in Carrara. This was to enable the Cardinal to commission a pietà for his own tomb. The result was an early example of a sculpted *pietà*, which is a representation of the crucified Christ on the lap of his mother. Although the subject was commonly painted in Italy, sculptural representations were more likely to be found in Germany and France. The idea probably originated from Germany in the fourteenth century and drew a parallel with the Madonna holding the infant Christ on her knee. One of the great problems with this composition was that the figure of Christ has to be at least as large as the Virgin if the proportions were to be realistic, and this led to difficulties in representing the Virgin properly supporting the dead Christ.

Michelangelo completed the sculpture in just one year. When the Cardinal died in August 1499, the *Pietà* was placed over his tomb in St. Peter's, Rome.

THE MADONNA OF THE MEADOW

Giovanni Bellini

This painting, made in about 1500 in Venice, shows the Madonna with the infant Christ on her lap and quite clearly demonstrates the compositional and religious parallels with the traditional *pietà* composition.

PIETÀ ATTRIBUTED TO
THE MASTER OF AVIGNON

This depiction of a pietà was made in Avignon, France, in about 1470 by an unknown artist. It owes more to the Gothic than the Renaissance style with its flat background and artificial decoration around the figures' heads, but it demonstrates the problem of comparative proportion between the Christ and Virgin. In this painting, the artist plays on the disparity by bending the figure of the dead Christ across the Virgin's lap, his unsupported legs and head adding to the sense of tragedy and pathos.

It is a measure of Michelangelo's genius that he was able to make the composition realistic without the viewer questioning the relative proportions of the Virgin and Christ. Michelangelo cleverly cloaked the Virgin's form in voluminous drapery, which disguised the fact that her lap is far too wide and that she would be far taller than her son if she were to stand. None of this matters, however, because the viewer is immediately captured by the pathos evoked by the work. The bowed head of the Virgin, partly cowled by her veil, and the outstretched arm with palm extended is infinitely expressive as she holds her dead son across her lap.

THE AUDIENCE FOR THE PICTURES

THE LAST JUDGMENT

The Sistine Chapel in Rome was built by Pope Sixtus IV in the 1470s as part of a building campaign to restore Rome after the papacy moved back there from Avignon, France. It stands about 131 feet high by 45 feet wide and originally had windows all around, six on each long wall, two on the altar wall and entrance wall. The chapel was painted by Michelangelo over a period of years and was completed in 1512. The altar wall originally had frescoes based on the Assumption of the Virgin, Baptism of Christ, and Finding of Moses. When Paul III became pope in 1534, he commissioned Michelangelo to paint a Last Judgment scene on the altar wall. The two altar wall windows were blocked up and Michelangelo's own frescoes were destroyed along

with those by other artists to make room for the new fresco, which would cover the entire wall.

In Michelangelo's painting the figure of Christ in the center with the figure of Mary just behind stands in judgment, holding up his hand to raise the dead ready for their ordeal.

Christ is surrounded by his saints, who all protest their sufferings and seek their rewards.

Figures rise from their graves on Christ's right, summoned by trumpeting angels.

The damned fall into hell on his left, driven on by Charon, the ferryman who takes the dead across the river Styx in his boat.

When Sebastiano del Piombo, who was in charge of making the wall ready had the wall prepared for oil painting, a furious Michelangelo argued that oil painting was fit only for women and lazy people. He had the surface removed and prepared again for fresco. When the painting was finally unveiled to Pope Paul III on October 31, 1541, it is said that he fell to his knees praying to God not to remember his sins on Judgment Day.

The Last Judgment reflects the change in fortunes of the Church and of Rome since the original Michelangelo commission to paint the ceiling over twenty years earlier. The apocalyptic painting covers an immense 45 by 40 feet. The invasion and ravage of Rome, which probably damaged the original frescoes in the chapel, and the destructive criticisms of the Church by the Reformation, had served to change the religious mood of the day into a darker and more somber one.

STORIES FROM THE LAST JUDGMENT

*P*ope Paul III understood and was supportive of Michelangelo's work, but many around him were openly critical of *The Last Judgment*. They said it was obscene and that "...the saints and angels, the former without any of the decency proper to this world, and the latter lacking any of the loveliness of Heaven... the genitals and organs of those in ecstasy in such relief that even in the whore-houses they couldn't fail to make one close one's eyes." In 1555 the new pope, Paul IV, who had been opposed to *The Last Judgment* painting from the start, asked Michelangelo to make the fresco "suitable."

Michelangelo replied: "Tell the Pope that this is a small matter and it can easily be made suitable; let him make the world a suitable place and painting will soon follow suit." Nevertheless, shortly after Michelangelo's death the fresco was "made suitable" by the addition of loincloths and other clothes, in some instances irreparably damaging the painting.

THE DAMNED

The judgment condemns the sinners to everlasting damnation in hell. Michelangelo's devils are in human form with only their coloring and claws distinguishing them from the humans they torment. What is so awesome about this vision is the way in which the condemned appear to be resigned to their fate, realizing for the first time that they are doomed and unable to resist. This is brilliantly achieved here by this detail of a man hiding his face and paralyzed with fear as he is dragged down into hell.

SELF-PORTRAIT

Michelangelo depicts himself as Saint Bartholomew astride a cloud, below and to the right of the central figure of a youthful Christ. The saints all hold an object symbolizing their martyrdom. Michelangelo holds out his flayed skin, perhaps also as a grim joke about his efforts in the cause of his art.

MINOS, PRINCE OF HELL

At some point during the painting
when the scaffolding was lowered,
Master of Ceremonies Biagio
da Cesena glimpsed the fresco,
even though Michelangelo was
most strict about not revealing
his work until it was ready.
Cesena complained to the pope
about the nude figures, which
he thought obscene. Cesena
wanted the pope to make
Michelangelo alter the
figures but the pope replied
that he had no jurisdiction
over hell. Michelangelo
was to get back at
Cesena by painting
his portrait as Minos,
prince of hell, shown
in the bottom right-hand corner of the fresco with a
serpent entwined about his waist.

ROSARY OF HOPE

This dead couple, having been awakened
from their graves and called to judgment,
cling to a rosary by which
they are being hauled up.
This may be a reference
to the need to adhere to
the true teachings of
the Church rather
than abandon it for
the heresy of the
Protestant faith, which
had abandoned the
rosary. This is a clue
to the message
of the fresco,
which not
only depicts
the last
judgment,
but may also
refer to the
Church and its
wicked and
corrupt ways,
which it was
now attempting
to change to
counter the attacks
it suffered during
the Reformation.

THE AUDIENCE FOR THE GREAT WORKS

GOLD FLORIN

Money has often been behind the creation of art.

The power of the great families such as the Medicis was absolute. They had amassed huge fortunes through banking and were very influential in the Church. The Florentine banks of the Medici years became the most important and powerful in Europe and allowed the family to become patrons of artists such as Michelangelo and Leonardo da Vinci, favorites of Lorenzo "the Magnificent" de'Medici. The Church was also enormously powerful, having been re-established in Rome. Its leading figures, such as Pope Julius II, were concerned with building the image of the Church. Julius II supported the Medicis of Florence and encouraged Florentine artists such as Michelangelo to work on the new projects he was planning for Rome. Julius II commissioned Bramante to build the Church of St. Peter's, which was to dominate the architecture of the city. The work of the great artists served to reinforce the power of the Church and its messages to a population whose life was centered on religion.

POPE JULIUS II *Raphael*

When Michelangelo completed the Sistine Chapel ceiling frescoes for Pope Julius II, they were admired by the people of Rome, who came crowding to see the spectacular sight. Julius thought that the paintings might be improved a little: "It must still be necessary to have it retouched with gold" was his comment, according to Vasari's book. Michelangelo's reply was: "I do not see that men should wear gold." The Pope continued: "It will look poor." Michelangelo answered by saying: "Those who are painted here were poor themselves."

THE LIFE OF MICHELANGELO

~1505~

Traveled to Rome to undertake a commission for Pope Julius II's tomb. Plans changed and Michelangelo was asked to paint the ceiling of the Sistine Chapel.

~1512~

Sistine Chapel finished and unveiled.

~1518~

Commissioned by Pope Leo to design the facade of the Medici family church of San Lorenzo in Florence, but the work was abandoned as money ran out.

~1524~

Designed and executed the Medici tombs.

~1527~

War in Rome as the Medicis were forced to flee and troops rampaged through the city. Michelangelo returned to Florence. His brother died of the plague.

~1531~

Michelangelo's father died.

~1535~

Michelangelo appointed sculptor and architect to the pope.

~1536~

Met Vittoria Colonna, the Marchioness of Pescara. They remained close until her death.

~1547~

Appointed architect of St. Peter's in Rome.

~1564~

Michelangelo died on February 18.

Circular paintings became popular in Italy in the fifteenth century (*tondo* is Italian for round); this one was commissioned by the Doni family in 1503. It depicts the Holy Family, with Mary reaching over her shoulder to take the infant Christ from Joseph. Michelangelo was asked to make the tondo for the wedding of Agnolo Doni and Maddalena Strozzi. It is said that when the painting was delivered, Agnolo Doni tried to settle for paying 40 ducats rather than the 70 ducats earlier agreed. Michelangelo threatened to take the painting back unless Doni paid twice the original sum, to which he eventually agreed.

PORTRAIT OF COSIMO DE'MEDICI

Pontormo

From 1434 Cosimo started to create his empire in Florence, constructing public buildings and commissioning artists. Lorenzo continued the family tradition when he came to power in 1469, six years before the birth of Michelangelo.

WHAT THE CRITICS SAY

O ne story has it that Michelangelo's rivals Bramante and Raphael conspired to get Michelangelo the commission for the Sistine Chapel frescoes knowing that he would refuse, as he considered himself a sculptor not a painter, and thereby would earn the disapproval of the pope and so be out of favor. How true this is we do not know, but this work is a lasting legacy upon which art historians and critics have heaped praise for centuries. Michelangelo is acknowledged as being instrumental in bringing about a change in the course of art. Not content with learning the techniques of art as a young apprentice, he strove to understand fully the complexity of the subject that fascinated him most: the human body. He even dissected corpses to be able to appreciate and represent the human form in any position or pose. This mastery earned him fame and wealth as rich merchants and popes competed for his services; it also elevated paintings and sculptures from the status of crafts to fine arts. Many historians credit Michelangelo with being the greatest sculptor, painter, and draftsman ever; he is an archetype of the artist as genius.

FAME IN PRINT

"From the hour when the Lord God, by His outstanding kindness, made me worthy not just of the presence (which I could scarcely have hoped to enter), but of the love, of the conversation and of the intimacy of Michelangelo Buonarroti, the unique sculptor and painter..."

So begins Vasari's uncritical biography of Michelangelo, and so begins the legend of Michelangelo the genius. Unlike any artist before him, Michelangelo was the subject of two biographies in his lifetime. Giorgio Vasari (shown above) published his *Lives of the Most Eminent Painters, Sculptors, and Architects* book in 1550, when Michelangelo was seventy-five years old. Three years later Ascanio Condivi published his *Life of Michelangelo*. The legend began in his lifetime and has continued for nearly 500 years.

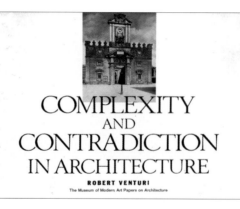

COMPLEXITY
AND
CONTRADICTION
IN ARCHITECTURE
ROBERT VENTURI
The Museum of Modern Art Papers on Architecture

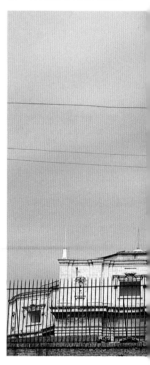

Today students and critics refer to the inventions of Michelangelo as one of the major influences on the course of Western architecture. (left)

FAME IN STONE

Pope Julius II had commissioned the architect Bramante to build a new church of St. Peter's in Rome. When Bramante died in 1514 the church was unfinished, and he left no plans or models for its

completion. Bramante's successors made no progress and Michelangelo was asked by Pope Paul III to take over the project in 1547. Michelangelo agreed to do it without payment for his spiritual good. He rejected the design of his predecessor, Sangello, criticizing it as "providing pasturage for sheep and oxen who know nothing of art." He came up with his own design, which he said was more faithful to Bramante's original, despite the fact that he and Bramante had been enemies. In return Sangello's supporters criticized Michelangelo to such an extent that the pope had to intervene.

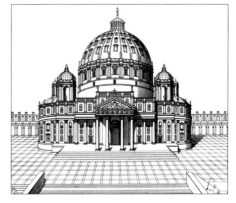

Michelangelo planned a hemispherical dome, as the drawing at the right shows. Building started in the late 1550s and halted when Michelangelo died in 1564. The drum upon which the dome sits is by Michelangelo's hand, but the dome's shape was changed by his successor, della Porta, who considered the hemisphere to lack stability and altered it to the more pointed shape that we see today. (above)

A LASTING IMPRESSION

THE CENTER OF POWER

Malevich

The power of Michelangelo's influence on artists of later generations is exemplified by a quote from the twentieth-century Russian Supremacist artist Kasimir Malevich. Malevich was among the first painters to work in a completely abstract idiom. He strove to achieve "the supremacy of pure feeling." To Malevich, the object was meaningless and the ideas of the conscious mind worthless. He said that the point at which the apex of a triangle touched the circumference of a circle was visually as powerful as the gap between the hand of God and the hand of Adam from Michelangelo's *The Creation of Adam*. Malevich was recognizing the compositional power of Michelangelo's art and trying to achieve it in his own, in purely abstract terms.

ichelangelo's influence on the course of Western art and architecture has been profound. The challenge of drawing the naked human form in complicated poses persists as a test for the would-be artist even today. The strength of Michelangelo's work lies in its ability to understand, imitate, and even surpass the classical masters, and to build on this by following his own spirit of invention. By influencing Italian art he influenced European art, and thereby art of the Western world. His buildings still dominate Rome today, and his sculptures and paintings are monumental milestones in the course of the history of art. Michelangelo considered himself to be a sculptor above all else. He believed his chisels released the sculpture from the stone. This famous sonnet was written in reply to Giovanni Strozzi who said that "the sculpture of Night for the Medici chapel tomb of Giuliano de'Medici was sculpted by an angel and would speak if awoken:"

"Caro m'e 'l sonno...
  Dear to me is sleep
  in stone while harm and
  shame persist;
  not to see, not to feel, is bliss;
  speak softly, do not wake me,
  do not weep."

This detail from *The Creation of Adam* has been used for all kinds of purposes such as advertising, films, television, and graphics. This is a testimony to its fame and everlasting endurance as an icon of five hundred years' standing.

During the latter part of his life, and continuing after his death, artists painting in the style of Michelangelo crowded their paintings with naked athletes. These pictures in the manner of Michelangelo imitated his style but missed the spirit of his work. This fashion has today became known as Mannerism. The fashion tended to elongate the human form, depicting it as a classical ideal, representing the figures in standard poses and portraying faces vacant of meaningful expression. Mannerist painters used intense colors to heighten emotional effect and the drama of the scene. El Greco was one of the most famous Mannerist painters.

The Trinity, El Greco

THE HEART OF ROME

The site of the Capitoline Hill, the civic center of ancient Rome, was rundown and medieval in appearance at the time of Michelangelo. Pope Paul III's plans to restore the site, known as the Piazza del Campidoglio, involved Michelangelo's designs for a remodeled square. The scheme was not finished until almost one hundred years after Michelangelo's death but is today a magnet for visitors to Rome. Its design reflects the ancient Roman tradition of *caput mundi*, the center of the world.

GLOSSARY

Classical - Classical or *classicism* is a type of art derived or supposed to be derived from the examples of Greek and Roman antiquity. Art from many different centuries referred to these early examples, which were thought to be of the highest standard.

Gothic - Usually refers to an architectural style developed between the twelfth and sixteenth centuries in Northern Europe, but also describes other art forms. The architectural style is tall, thin, spiky, and decorative.

Mannerism - A term used today to describe some types of art that followed the Renaissance but that broke the rules of classical art. Mannerist painters tended to stretch and elongate the human form and use vivid colors to emphasize emotion.

Pantheon - The circular temple in Rome dedicated to all the Roman gods. Originally built in 27 B.C. and subsequently rebuilt and used for Christian worship. The Roman temple was based on earlier Greek temples.

Proportion - How one part of a painting, sculpture, or building relates to the other parts. Many artists sought to define proportion in terms of the human body, for example, calculating that the head must always be one-seventh of the total height of the figure.

Trompe l'oeil - Translates from the French as *deceives the eye*. An effect used in painting that deceives the viewer into thinking that what is painted is actually real. It is often used for comical effect; for example, painting a fly on a picture frame.

ACKNOWLEDGEMENTS

ticktock Publishing, LTD UK would like to thank: Graham Rich, Tracey Pennington, and Peter Done for their assistance.

Acknowledgments: Picture Credits t=top, b=bottom, c=center, l=left, r=right, OFC=outside front cover, IFC=inside front cover, IBC= inside back cover, OBC= outside back cover.

Photo © AKG London/Erich Lessing; 6tl. © Ancient Art & Architecture Collection; 2/3cb, 14tr. Ashmolean Museum, Oxford; 9tl. Bargello, Florence/Bridgeman Art Library, London; OBC & 26tl. Copyright © British Museum; 15cb. Collegium Maius, Cracow, Poland. Photo © AKG London/Erich Lessing; 3br. Cappella Medici, Florence/Bridgeman Art Library, London; 14br, 15tr. Casa Buonarroti, Florence/Bridgeman Art Library, London; IFC/1. Mary Evans Picture Library; 2bl, 3tr, 28tl. Galleria degli Uffizi, Florence. Photo © AKG London/Erich Lessing; 7br, 27cb. Galleria degli Uffizi, Florence/Bridgeman Art Library, London; 8bl, 27tl. Galleria dell'Accademia, Florence. Photo © AKG London; OBC & 3c. Galleria dell'Accademia, Florence. Photo © AKG London/Erich Lessing; 18/19c. Galleria dell'Accademia, Florence/Bridgeman Art Library, London; OFCl, OBC & 5cb, OBC & 18tl, 19tr, OBC & 19br. Galleria dell'Accademia, Florence/Lauros-Giraudon/Bridgeman Art Library, London; 17tr. Chris Gray; 5tl, 28/29cb, 30/31cb. Kunsthistorisches Museum, Vienna. Photo © AKG London/Erich Lessing; 5tr. Musee du Louvre, Paris. Photo © AKG London/Erich Lessing; 7cl, 21tr. Museo dell'Opera del Duomo, Florence. Photo © AKG London/Erich Lessing; 8tl. Museum fur Volkerkunde, Berlin/Bridgeman Art Library, London; 2tl. By courtesy of the Trustees of The National Gallery, London; 20bl. National Gallery, London. Photo © AKG London; 26bl. National Maritime Museum, London; 3tl. Palazzo Medici-Riccardi, Florence. Photo © AKG London; 4bl. Private Collection/Bridgeman Art Library, London; 30tl. Prado, Madrid/Bridgeman Art Library, London; 31tr. © Ronald Sheridan/Ancient Art & Architecture Collection; 29t. Sistine Chapel, Vatican, Rome. Photo © AKG London; 22/23. St. Peter's, Vatican/Bridgeman Art Library, London; 20/21c. Stanza della Segnatura, Vatican, Rome. Photo © AKG London/Erich Lessing; 7tr. Unterlindenmuseum, Colmar. Photo © AKG London/Erich Lessing; 6bl. Vatican Museums and Galleries, Rome/Bridgeman Art Library, London; OFCr, 9cb, 10/11, 12t & 30cr, OBC & 12/13cb, 13tr, 24tl, 24/25c, 25tr, 25br.

BARRON'S